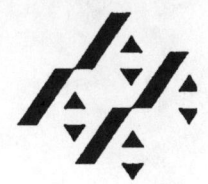

D1742936

ATLAS
1 Workbook
Learning-Centered Communication

Angela Llanas

Libby Williams

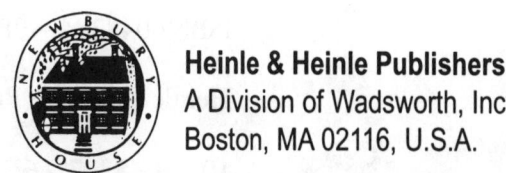

Heinle & Heinle Publishers
A Division of Wadsworth, Inc.
Boston, MA 02116, U.S.A.

Illustrations
Ruth Flanigan: pps. 1; 3(bottom); 4; 9 (top right, middle); 12 (top); 13 (top); 14; 20; 22; 23; 25; 30; 31; 34; 43 (top); 45; 49.
Marcy Ramsey: pps. 5; 6; 9 (bottom); 10 (top); 11; 12; 13 (bottom); 15; 16; 26; 28; 35; 36; 38; 39; 43 (bottom); 46; 48.

Photographs
pps. 2 Kent Bailey/Tony Stone Images; 3 (top) Frank Siteman/Stock Boston; 9 (top left) Peter Correz/Tony Stone Images; 10 (middle) Dan Bosler/Tony Stone Images; 21 Michael McGovern/The Picture Cube; 37 Jon Riley/Tony Stone Images; 57 (top) Charles Trainer/The Miami Herald; 57 (middle) Magnum Photos, Inc.; 57 (bottom) AP/Wide World Photos.

Photo Research: Sharon Donahue

The publication of ATLAS was directed by the members of the Heinle & Heinle Global Innovations Publishing Team:

Elizabeth Holthaus, ESL Team Leader
David C. Lee, Editorial Director
John F. McHugh, Market Development Director
Lisa McLaughlin, Production Editor
Nancy Mann, Developmental Editor

Also participating in the publication of the program were:

Publisher: Stanley J. Galek
Assistant Editor: Kenneth Mattsson
Manufacturing Coordinator: Mary Beth Hennebury
Full Service Design and Production: LeGwin Associates

Copyright © 1995 by Heinle & Heinle Publishers

All rights reserved. No part of this publication may be reproduced or transmitted in any form or by any means, electronic or mechanical, including photocopying, recording, or any information storage and retrieval system, without permission in writing from the publisher.

Manufactured in the United States of America.

ISBN: 0–8384–4089–4

Heinle & Heinle Publishers is a division of Wadsworth, Inc.

10 9 8 7 6 5 4 3 2 1

Contents

1

Getting to Know You

1 Which word doesn't belong?

Example: women   male   (book)   people

1. English   Japanese   Spanish   Chile
2. pencil   pen   speak   book
3. family   listen   practice   read
4. France   Korean   Brazil   China
5. you   she   what   I

2 Use your dictionary to find out what countries people of these nationalities are from:

Example: Polish   *Poland*

1. Italian _____
2. Dutch _____
3. Peruvian _____
4. Irish _____
5. Egyptian _____
6. Indian _____
7. Malaysian _____

3 Invent a new name and nationality for yourself.

A Write your invented name and nationality here:

Last name: _____

First name(s): _____

Nationality: _____

B Now ask someone else to invent a new name and nationality. Complete the blanks below with your partner's invented information.

Last name: _____

First name(s): _____

Nationality: _____

C Read this report:

I interviewed Jane Anne Cook. She is English.

D Write a similar report on the person you interviewed.

_____

4 A 🎧 Listen to the cassette and complete the information about this pop star.

Last name: _____

First name: _____

Professional name: _____

Nationality: _____

B Now complete this biographical extract on Rick Rocker from *Top Pop* magazine.

Rocker is Rick's professional _____.
His real _____ name is O'Reilly. Rick
Rocker is _____. He is Ireland's
newest pop star.

❺ A Fill in the blanks in this conversation at school.

Teacher: Hello. _____ you a new student here?

Student: Yes, I _____.

Teacher: _____ is your last _____?
Student: Wilson.

Teacher: And your _____ _____?
Student: Brian.

Teacher: Where _____ _____ from?
Student: Toronto, Canada.
Teacher: Welcome.

B Fill in the blanks.

1. A: Hello, I _____ Tom.   B: Hi, _____ to meet you.

2. A: _____ you Michael?   B: Yes, I _____.

3. A: What_____ your name?   B: My name's Paul.

4. A: Are _____ Anne and Tony?   B: Yes, they _____.

5. A: _____ she Mexican?   B: _____, she isn't. She's Peruvian.

6. They _____ French.

7. A: _____ you from Korea?   B: Yes, _____ am.

8. A: What's her nationality?   B: _____ is Japanese.

❻ A Look at the flags. Unscramble the letters. What are the countries?

RUTYEK   RIS ANKLA   NDLAWTISREZ   MAJICAA   SUTALIAAR   DENWES   YAKEN   ZNVUEEEAL

B Match the cities with the countries. Use an atlas if necessary. Write about the people like this:

Anne is from Canberra. She's Australian.

Bern	Stockholm	Nairobi	Canberra	Colombo
Kingston	Ankara	Caracas		

2 This Is My Sister

1 **A** Use a dictionary to find out what these words mean.

cousin, niece, aunt, grandmother, relations, uncle, grandson, nephew, grandfather, granddaughter

B Using the new words, find out about Henry Fitzwilliam Junior's relatives. Write under each name the person's relationship to Henry Fitzwilliam Junior.

❷ 🎧 Listen to the conversation between a man and a female employee of Key Rent-a-Car. Fill in the form.

KEY **RENT-A-CAR**

Last name: _____

First name: _____

Address: _____

Telephone number: _____

License number: _____

❸ A Read this conversation. In groups of four, act out a similar conversation. Change names, relationships, and countries.

Hello, I'm Maria.

Hi, I'm Kate.

This is my husband, Sam.

Nice to meet you.

And this is my boyfriend, Juan.

Where are you from?

Kate is from the United States, and I'm from Cuba.

We are from England.

Where are you from?

B Now write your conversation.

4 **A** Look at the photograph of Joe's family. Read his explanation and then write in the names.

Petra			

> This is my wife. Her name is Petra. Our children are Christie and Paul. Petra is Russian. This is Katia, her sister, with her boyfriend, Juan. He is from Mexico. And this is his dog, Napoleon. Here is Fred. Fred is my brother, and that is Sandra, his wife. This is their daughter, Lizzie. I am not in the photograph.

B Now complete this conversation with Joe.

Friend: Is this your wife?
Joe: Yes, it is.

Friend: What's _____ name?
Joe: Petra.

Friend: Where _____ _____ from?

Joe: _____ is _____ _____.

Friend: Are these _____ children?

Joe: Yes, _____ are.

Friend: What _____ _____ names?
Joe: Christie and Paul.

Friend: _____ Katia's boyfriend _____ Russia?

Joe: No, he isn't. ____ _____ from Mexico.

Friend: Is this _____ dog?

Joe: Yes, it is. _____ name is Napoleon.
Friend: Is Fred your friend?

Joe: No, he isn't. He is _____ brother, and here are _____ wife and daughter, Sandra and Lizzie.
Friend: You all look happy.

Joe: Yes, _____ are all very happy in the photo.

❺ Fill in the words in these sentences and circle them in the puzzle.

```
E  F  D  D  V (H) C  W  W  R
L  A  D  D  R (E) S  S  1  C
U  M  Y  O  U (R) I  A  F  F
Z  I  C  J  A  F  S  K  E  B
K  L  Y  F  W  R  T  A  W  H
M  Y  I  R  B  X  E  Q  P  I
F  E  H  O  O  U  R  A  W  S
J  P  J  M  W  H  E  R  E  Y
D  O  E  B  T  H  E  I  R  A
P  H  O  T  O  G  R  A  P  H
```

1. This is Lourdes and __her__ friend, Marcela.

2. Where is Mari _____? From Prague.

3. What's your _____? It's 15 Gordon Street.

4. What do you _____? I'm a dentist.

5. I have two brothers and one _____.

6. _____ do you live? In Buenos Aires.

7. I have six brothers and four sisters. We're a big _____.

8. This is a _____ of George and Tina and _____ dog, Spot.

9. We are Mary and James Penn, and _____ phone number is 278-8800.

10. What's your name? _____ name is Frantz.

11. James is from New York. _____ address is 124 Harvard Boulevard.

12. What is _____ last name? My last name is Williams.

13. This is Mr. Shaw and his _____, Mrs. Shaw.

❻ Choose a famous person (the leader of a country, a member of royalty, a pop singer, etc.). Find out about the person's family. On a separate sheet of paper, draw the famous person's family tree and write eight sentences about the person's family.

3 What Do You Do?

1 Answer the clues to solve the occupation puzzle.

ACROSS

1. They work in a restaurant. They are _____.

2. Put these letters in the correct order and find an occupation: CUOTCANTNA.

3. She works in a hospital. She's a _____.

4. _____ work in hospitals with doctors.

5. Put these letters in the correct order and find an occupation: WRYALE.

6. She works with a newspaper. She's a _____.

DOWN

1. Tom Cruise is an _____.

2. She works in a school. She's a _____.

3. Unscramble the letters to find an occupation: NERDAC.

4. We are in Paris with a RUOT UIDGE.

5. Elizabeth Taylor is a _____ _____.

6. A _____ flies planes.

Mr. Dealberg, the famous film director, is looking at this photograph. The man in the photo is just the person he wants for a big role in his next film. Read the passage and answer Mr. Dealberg's questions.

This is a photograph of Jimmy Burton. Jimmy Burton is an actor. But he isn't a very experienced actor. Most days, in the mornings he looks for work in the theater.

"I'm really interested in acting!" Jimmy told our reporter. "But it sure is difficult!"

"So what do you do for money?" the reporter asked Jimmy.

"Every evening, I work here at Billy's Burgers. I'm a very experienced waiter!" he laughed.

What's this man's name?
_____
What's his occupation?
_____
Where does he work?
_____
Is he an experienced actor?
_____

 Work in pairs. Student A looks at Box A, and student B looks at Box B on page 10. Ask questions and fill in the missing information in your box.

Look at number 1. What's his name? What does he do? Where does he work?

BOX A

1.	2.	3.	4.	5.	6.
Name:	Name:	Names:	Name: *Sadie Guzman*	Names: *John and Clark Simpson*	Name: *Harold Jones*
Occupation:	Occupation:	Occupations:	Occupation: *Teacher*	Occupation: *Waiters*	Occupation: *Engineer*
Place of employment:	Place of employment:	Places of employment:	Place of employment: *Area high school*	Place of employment: *The Rib Eye Steak House*	Place of employment: *IBM*

BOX B

1.	2.	3.	4.	5.	6.
Name: David Wright	Name: Tracy Goodman	Names: Susan and Phillip Scott	Name:	Names:	Name:
Occupation: Teller	Occupation: Dancer	Occupations: Doctors	Occupation:	Occupation:	Occupation:
Place of employment: Bank of America	Place of employment: The Blue Bird Night Club	Places of employment: Jersey City Hospital	Place of employment:	Place of employment:	Place of employment:

4 Listen to Charlotte White talking about herself and complete the paragraph.

What do I _____? Well, I'm a _____ in the morning. I teach _____ at the Chicago Language Center. I'm a _____, too. I _____ to night school. I _____ computer programming. On _____ I go out with my boyfriend. His _____ Gary. Gary _____ in a restaurant. _____ a chef.

5 Using your dictionary, place the words in the box under the correct column.

lawyer	pilot	painter	doctor
_____	_____	_____	_____
_____	_____	_____	_____
_____	_____	_____	_____

airport	client	gallery	plane	case	patient
jury	canvas	brush	X-ray	passenger	operation

❻ A Fill in the blanks.

1. On Sunday afternoons, I _____ tennis.

2. What _____ they do in the mornings? _____ go to school.

3. _____ you play football? No, I _____ .

4. _____ she watch TV in the evenings? No, she _____.

5. What _____ you do? We _____ chefs. We work in a restaurant.

B Write questions to these answers.

1. _____? He's a lawyer.

2. _____? No, she isn't. She's a doctor.

3. _____? I'm a journalist.

4. _____? They are salesclerks.

5. _____? No, I'm not. I'm a teacher.

❼ Look at these pictures. What professions do they show? Write some sentences about the work three of these people do.

| Olga Ivanovich | Mario Spinelli | Sharon Chang | Davy Jones | John Flannegan | Wilmer Washington |

_____

_____

_____

_____

_____

_____

_____

_____

_____

_____

4 What Are You Wearing?

1 What are the articles of clothing in the puzzle?

2 Look at the picture and complete these sentences with words from the puzzle.

Film star Joshua Robbins is seen here arriving at the Los Angeles Charity Ball. But who is Joshua's mystery girlfriend? That's a secret! Whoever the mystery lady is, she certainly is beautiful, with big green eyes and long blond hair. The mystery lady is wearing a long black evening _____ with diamond-studded _____ on her feet. She is wearing a white silk _____ and has a long silver-colored _____around her neck. Joshua isn't half as elegant as the mystery lady. Is this what film stars are wearing at charity balls these days? As you can see, Joshua is wearing old blue _____ with an old sports _____ on top of a _____. And he has _____ on his feet! Joshua is wearing an old college _____ around his neck! Well, it looks like Joshua is wearing a costume to the Los Angeles Charity Ball.

❸ A 🎧 Listen to the conversation. Two teams are playing a guessing game. Look at the picture. Which team wins, the women or the men? How many questions do they ask?

_____

_____

_____

_____

_____

_____

_____

B In the space provided near the picture, write a description of what the man is wearing.

C Play the game. Get into teams. Each team draws a picture of their person. Choose from Boxes A and B. The other team tries to guess in 12 questions.

The Clothes
jacket
blouse
dress
pants
jeans
skirt
shoes
sneakers
sweater

Draw your person here

The Colors
green
brown
white
grey
red
pink
blue

❹ A Read the paragraph and name the people.

Lassie

Once a year, Mr. and Mrs. Simpson organize a costume party for their son, Sam. This year the party is at Mrs. Simpson's sister's house. Sam is wearing a big cardboard box. Sam's brother's name is William. He is wearing his father's cowboy boots. Sam's school friends are John and Jason. They are wearing white sheets. Sam's cousins' costumes are beautiful. Sheila is wearing a dancer's costume and her mother's shoes. Ellen is wearing her grandmother's hat. Sam's friends' dog is by the door. She is wearing dark glasses. Her name is Lassie.

B Fill in the blanks in these sentences about the party. Try this without looking at the paragraph.

1. Is the party at Mrs. _____ house? Yes, it is.

2. What _____? A cardboard box.

3. Are _____ school friends _____ white sheets? Yes, _____.

4. Sam's _____ name is William.

5. What is William wearing? He _____.

6. _____ Jason and John _____ cowboy boots? No, _____.

7. What is Sheila wearing? _____.

8. Sam's _____ dog is _____ dark glasses.

5 Look at these adjectives. What are their opposites? Use your dictionary to find the words you don't know.

big   _____
blond   _____
beautiful   _____
short   _____
kind   _____
slim   _____
white   _____

6 Using your dictionary, find the English words for the following items of clothing:

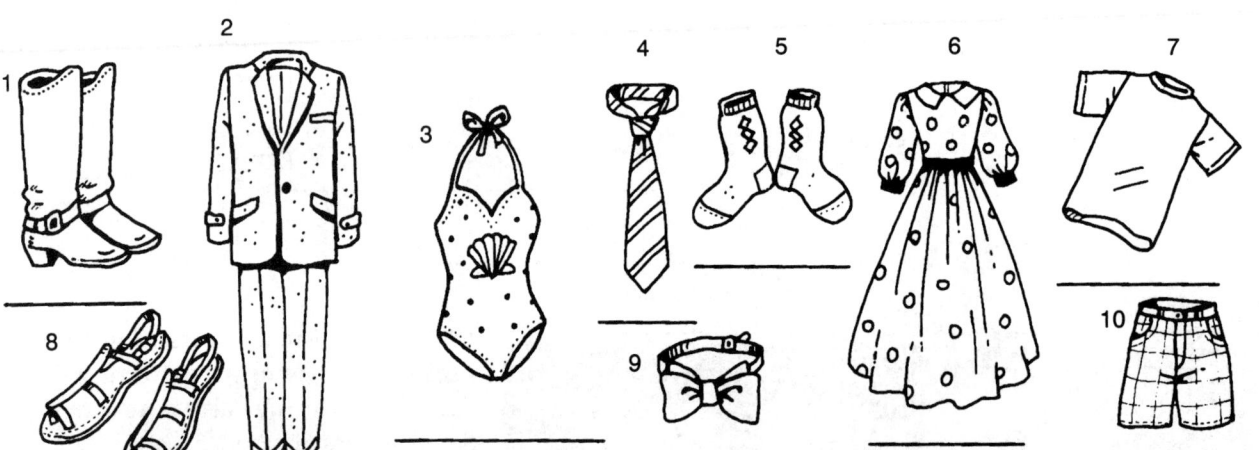

7 Cut a picture out of a magazine and describe what the people are wearing. (See the paragraph on Joshua and his mystery girlfriend.) Use your dictionary for words you don't know.

DERBY AND JOAN

1 Read the story. Use your dictionary if necessary. Then do the activity that follows the story.

Mr. Derby is an elderly gentleman. He is a widower. He comes from New York. He's tall and thin with thick white hair and a gray moustache. Mr. Derby loves the park. He goes there every afternoon. He takes a bag of bread because he likes to feed the ducks.

Mrs. Emerson is a widow. She's small and plump and wears glasses. She has a kind smile. Like Mr. Derby, Mrs. Emerson comes from New York. She loves books. She goes to the park every afternoon and sits in the sun reading a book.

Right now, Mr. Derby is sitting on a bench by the lake. He's watching the ducks. Mrs. Emerson is sitting on the bench, too. She's reading a book. It's a lovely day. The sun is shining. Mrs. Emerson is closing her book.

Mr. Derby: Hello, ma'am. What a lovely day!
Mrs. Emerson: Yes, it sure is.
Mr. Derby: Excuse me, ma'am. What's your name?
Mrs. Emerson: Joan. . . Joan Emerson.
Mr. Derby: And I'm Edward Derby.
Mrs. Emerson: I'm very pleased to meet you, Mr. Derby.
Mr. Derby: It's a pleasure to meet you. What are you reading there?
Mrs. Emerson: It's a novel. . . . It's called *Meeting by the Swans*. Why are you laughing?
Mr. Derby: Well, ma'am, we're meeting . . . but we're meeting by the ducks, not the swans.

The sun is going down. Mr. Derby and Mrs. Emerson are still sitting on the bench in the park, but Mr. Derby isn't watching the ducks, and Mrs. Emerson isn't reading her book. They're talking. It's a beautiful evening for a talk in the park.

Match these phrases to the correct person:

      Mr. Derby   *Mrs. Emerson*

_____   _____

_____   _____

_____   _____

_____   _____

has gray hair	wears glasses
has a kind smile	is tall
loves reading	likes feeding the ducks
loves the park	is plump

CHECK YOUR PROGRESS

❷ Match the questions with the answers.

1. What is Rosa's last name?	a. I'm a doctor.
2. Is that your parents' house?	b. No, I'm not.
3. Are you Mexican?	c. No, I don't.
4. What do you do?	d. Blue pants and a white sweater.
5. What is he wearing?	e. Yes, he does.
6. What do they do in the evening?	f. Yes, they are.
7. Do you play tennis?	g. Yes, it is.
8. What does she do?	h. They have dinner.
9. Does he read books?	i. She's a teacher.
10. Are they wearing jeans?	j. Moreno.

❸ Write the questions.

1. _____? I'm from Melbourne, Australia.

2. _____? She's wearing a blue skirt and red blouse.

3. _____? She's a doctor.

4. _____? In the evenings? I read.

4   Write true answers to these questions.

1. What are you wearing? _____

2. Are you from France?   _____

3. Are you studying German now? _____

4. Do you play baseball on Saturdays?_____

5. What's your best friend's name? _____

6. What's your nationality? _____

5   Fill in the blanks in this conversation.

Dottie: Hi, I'm Dottie. What's _____?

Boris: I'm Boris. Hi.

Dottie: _____?

Boris: I'm from Leningrad, but I _____ in California.

Dottie: Tell me about your _____.

Boris: I have a brother and two sisters.

Dottie: What _____?

Boris: _____ is an actor, and my two sisters _____ doctors.

Dottie: What's _____ name? Is he famous?

Boris: His name is Ivan, and no, he _____ famous.

Dottie: And, Boris, what _____?

Boris: I'm an engineer. Why are you asking so many questions?

Dottie: Because I'm a _____. I _____ for the *Daily News*.

6 Fill in the words in these sentences, and find them in the puzzle.

1. She is from Chile. She's _____.

2. His last name is Smith and his _____ name is John.

3. _____ do you do? I'm an artist.

4. Is she French? No, she _____ Korean.

5. This is my brother. _____ name is Miguel.

6. _____ you like hockey?

7. _____ Mary work in a hospital?

8. Are they Carlos and Maria? Yes, they _____.

9. Is she Anna? Yes, _____ is.

10. Mr. Nakamura has two sons and one _____.

11. Are _____ wearing jeans? Yes, I am.

12. He is a _____. He works in a school.

13. We are not studying French. We are studying _____.

14. The man is wearing _____ and a shirt. The _____ is wearing a skirt and a sweater.

15. What are your occupation, address, and _____?

```
F  W  D  O  X  E  N  G  L  I  S  H
1  H  J  K  P  Y  A  F  D  S  A  T
R  A  S  Q  Z  X  T  M  N  P  P  E
S  T  H  X  C  H  I  L  E  A  N  A
T  X  E  B  M  W  O  M  A  N  D  C
D  O  E  S  I  Q  N  Y  O  T  P  H
W  Q  V  T  M  T  A  J  H  S  G  E
A  R  E  V  D  F  L  R  T  Y  P  R
A  Q  Q  W  V  C  I  X  B  N  M  M
I  D  A  U  G  H  T  E  R  I  I  I
H  I  S  Z  X  S  Y  O  U  M  I  S
```

6 Do You Like Jazz?

1 Find the hidden word (1 DOWN). Do you like going to this place?

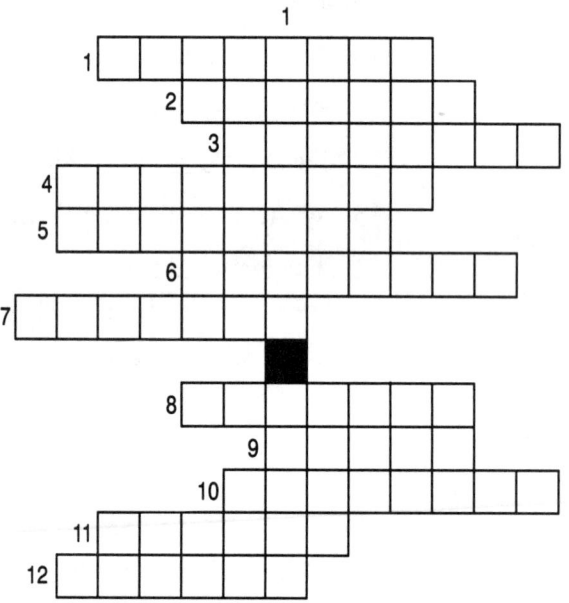

1. The Blue Jays in Canada and the Yankees in the United States are

   famous _____ teams.

2. We like _____.

3. She doesn't like _____.

4. I like _____.

5. Do you like _____?

6. Guns and Roses are giving two _____.

7. He goes _____ on Saturday evenings.

8. They don't like _____.

9. He likes eggs for breakfast and pizza for _____.

10. I don't like _____ the house.

11. We like the _____.

12. He plays _____ on Saturday mornings.

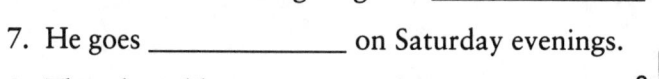

This is Lee Kopek. Lee works for a well-known university in the United States. She's the Housing Officer. Lee helps students to find housing. Most first-year students like to share rooms with other students when they first go to college. It's Lee's job to help them find other students with the same likes and dislikes, so they will be happy sharing a room. Lee likes her job. "It's a great job!" she says. "I meet a lot of really interesting kids."

A Are these statements true or false? Circle T (True) or F (False).

1. Lee Kopek is a university student. T F

2. Lee helps students to find rooms to live in. T F

3. Most first-year students don't like sharing rooms. T F

4. Lee dislikes her job. T F

B When Lee interviews a new student, she makes notes about his or her likes and dislikes. Here are some pages from Lee's notebook. With a partner, decide which students would be happy sharing a room.

Name: *Guadalupe Ramiréz*
Nationality: *Mexican*
Likes: *Cooking, shopping, fashionable clothes*
Dislikes: *Sports*

Name: *Ana Do Nascimento*
Nationality: *Portuguese*
Likes: *Pop music, movies, parties*
Dislikes: *TV, taking part in organized sports*

Name: *Marie Dupont*
Nationality: *French Canadian*
Likes: *Ice skating, traveling, reading*
Dislikes: *Cooking, dancing, TV*

Name: *Jennifer King*
Nationality: *African American*
Likes: *Reading, classical music, playing the piano*
Dislikes: *Pop music, discos*

Name: *Roberta Fares*
Nationality: *Brazilian*
Likes: *Watching soccer on TV, cooking, reading travel books*
Dislikes: *Parties, movies*

Name: *Pamela Lemonde*
Nationality: *French*
Likes: *Disco dancing, rock concerts, buying CDs*
Dislikes: *All types of sports*

Name: *Diana Finch*
Nationality: *English*
Likes: *Playing the flute, serious movies, TV documentaries*
Dislikes: *Dancing, noisy parties*

Name: *Sofia Bertonini*
Nationality: *Haitian*
Likes: *Shopping, designing her own clothes, disco dancing*
Dislikes: *Cooking, movies about American football, boxing, etc.*

C Write your decisions here:

Freshman shared housing

1. Pamela Lemonde and _____ because

_____

2. _____ and _____ because

_____

3. _____ and _____ because

_____

4. _____ and _____ because

_____

❸ 🎧 Listen to the conversation with two tourists in the United States on the cassette and fill out the chart to show Hans's and Lisel's likes and dislikes.

	Hans		Lisel	
	likes	*dislikes*	*likes*	*dislikes*
food		✓		
clothes				
people				
music				
shopping				

❹ Using your dictionary, match the drawings with the correct word.

(a)

(b)

(c)

(d)

(e)

(f)

(g)

(h)

(i)

(j)

(k)

(l)

(m)

(n)

_____ watch

_____ water skis

_____ saucepan

_____ tent

_____ ring

_____ earrings

_____ chair

_____ necklace

_____ table

_____ blender

_____ tennis racquet

_____ toaster

_____ bread knife

_____ bed

In which stores would you find the things on the previous page?

THE KITCHEN CORNER   MIKE'S SPORTS CENTER   THE JEWELRY CENTER   SMITH'S FURNITURE STORE

saucepan _____   _____   _____   _____

_____   _____   _____   _____

_____   _____   _____   _____

_____   _____   _____   _____

_____   _____   _____   _____

❺ What time is it? Write the time in words.

(a)    (b)    (c)    (d)

_____   _____   _____   _____

❻ Fill in the blanks.

1. What time _____ the movie start?

2. I _____ classical music, but I don't like rock music. _____ about you?

3. _____ you like movies? No, I _____.

4. _____ Paul like hockey? Yes, he _____.

5. Tom _____ swimming, but he doesn't like football.

6. We _____ cooking, but we _____ _____ cleaning.

7. _____ Juan and Yokio like baseball? Yes, ____ _____.

8. _____ is it? It's ten after three.

7 World time: Find out what time it is in the following towns when it is 7 A.M. (GMT) in London.

1. Tokyo _____

2. Sidney _____

3. New Delhi _____

4. Mexico City _____

5. Santiago de Chile _____

6. Teheran _____

7. Washington _____

8. Your city (if it's not on the list) _____

7 Coffee to Go

1 A Read the clues and find out what the words 1–5 ACROSS are. What is the word 1 DOWN?

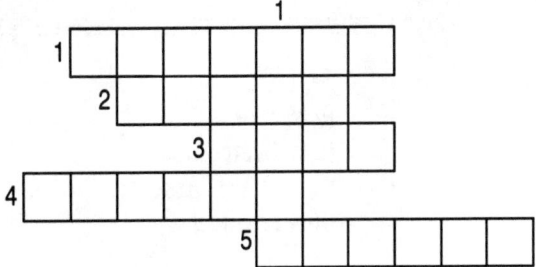

ACROSS

1. Unscramble these letters—DRCAHED—and you have a type of cheese.

2. This is very like number 3, but it is thicker. Some people like it in coffee or on strawberries.

3. This comes from cows. Children drink a lot of it.

4. This is yellow. It is usually spread on bread or toast. You need it for making most cakes, too.

5. This is made from milk. You can buy it in different fruit flavors. Many people like it for breakfast. It is very nutritious.

6. What is number 1 DOWN? _____.

B Write a puzzle like this one on one of the other food groups, and try it out on a friend.

2 A You use all of these things when you're eating or drinking. What are they called in English? Use your dictionary if necessary.

B Using your dictionary, find words for kitchen equipment. Did the other people in the class find different words? Add them to your list.

microwave

_____

_____

_____

_____

_____

_____

3 🎧 Carla and Frank are at a restaurant. Look at the menu. Listen to the conversation. Write *C* by what Carla chooses and *F* by what Frank chooses.

SOUPS	**SALADS**
Red Bean Soup	Green Salad
Iced Beetroot Soup	Tomato Salad
Carrot Vichyssoise	Caesar Salad
Cheese Soup	
Chilled Avocado Soup	**DESSERTS**
	Apple Tart and Cream
MAIN DISHES	Banana Delight
Casserole of Beef	Fruit Salad
Roast Duck	Orange Sherbet
Steak (served with fries)	Lemon Soufflé
Chicken Supreme	Nut and Chocolate Cake
Hamburger	
Stuffed Peppers	
Virginia Ham	

4 A Read this conversation. Practice it with a partner.

Cheese and salami pizza:
200 grams cheese
1 large pizza dough
20 slices of salami
2 tomatoes

B Now have a similar conversation with your partner. You want to prepare some food for a party. Student A looks at information box A below. Student B looks at the information box B on page 65.

INFORMATION BOX A

You want to make a yogurt fruit dessert. This is what you need. Find out if your partner has the ingredients.

400 grams natural yogurt
4 cups of granola
4 apples
3 bananas
2 teaspoons of brown sugar

This is what you have in your refrigerator:

20 slices of bread
1 stick of butter
100 grams of cheese
5 tomatoes

5 Complete the sentences with an appropriate word or phrase from this list:

a lot of	enough	how much	how many

1. _____ apples are there in the refrigerator? There are six.

2. _____ sugar do you want? Just a little.

3. Is there _____ granola for six of us? No, there isn't.

4. There are _____ calories in a pizza.

5. _____ eggs does he want? He wants two.

6. There isn't _____ cheese for this sandwich.

7. _____ yogurt is there in the refrigerator?

8. Help yourself! There is _____ popcorn on the table.

6 Read this passage and write the questions for the answers that follow.

Giovanni Toscani is a master chef. There are always a lot of movie stars at his restaurant in San Francisco. Giovanni Toscani prepares nutritious low-calorie food. There's no junk food at his restaurant! It's all healthful (and expensive!).

There are a lot of famous people here tonight. Joshua Robbins is here with some friends. He's having a party to celebrate the opening of his latest film.

"Joshua, do you like the food here?"

"Oh yes! I always eat here. Giovanni's food is so healthy, and I have to watch my weight!"

But wait. Here comes Giovanni. This is a surprise! Giovanni is . . . well . . . big!

"How much do you weigh, Giovanni?"

"Two hundred thirty pounds. I think healthy food is unhealthy! Fruit juice and salad are not enough for me. I don't eat what I cook! I eat at the restaurant across the street."

"So what do you have for lunch, Giovanni?"

"I have a couple of pepperoni pizzas with double cheese and a plate of spaghetti. And a bottle of red wine. Saluti!"

Example: ___*What's the chef's name*___ ?
His name is Giovanni Toscani.

1. _____ ? It's in San Francisco.

2. _____ ? It's all healthy.

3. _____ ? He's having a party.

4. _____ ? 230 pounds.

5. _____ ? He has a couple.

7 Using an encyclopedia or other reference book, choose a part of the world and find out what people eat or drink there. Write about it.

8 Can You Swim?

1 There is a musical instrument in the puzzle (1 DOWN). What is it?

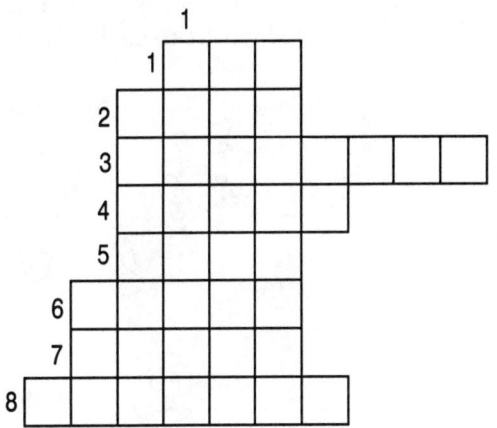

CLUES

1. _____ they swim? Yes, they can.

2. Can you _____ the guitar?

3. Who is your _____ comedy actor?

4. Who can _____ a car?

5. He can't play a musical instrument, but he can _____ .

6. Who can tell a _____ story for the evening's entertainment?

7. He can _____ four languages.

8. Is Jenny playing squash? No, she is _____ weights.

2 Use your dictionary to fill in the gaps in this paragraph with the words in the box.

fires	stunt man	break	shark	moving
dangerous	leg	high	helicopter	brave

Joshua Robbins, the movie star, is working on a new action film, "The Accident." The movie company doesn't want him to _____ an arm or a _____. That would cost the company thousands of dollars. So, in the film, Joshua doesn't do the _____ scenes. Who does them for him? A _____. His name is Mick McMan. Mick is _____ and highly trained. He can fall off _____ buildings. He can jump out of _____ cars. He can run through _____. In "The Accident," he falls out of a _____ and fights a _____. You can see the movie soon.

3 🎧 Look at the following drawings and listen to the conversation on the cassette. The producer of the TV program "America's Most Talented Pets" is talking to two pet owners who want to be on the show with their pets, Spot and Toby. Which pet can do which trick? Put an *S* for Spot or a *T* for Toby next to each drawing. Which pet would you choose for the show?

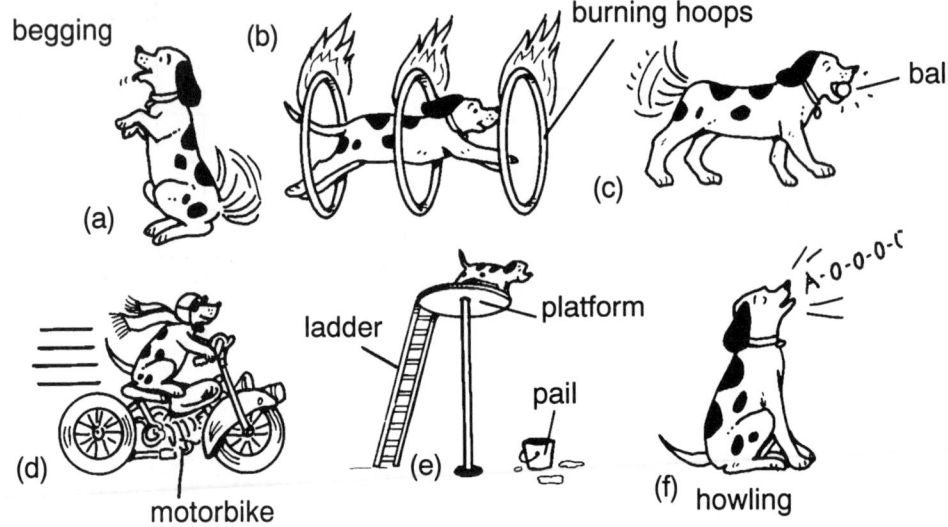

begging (a)
(b) burning hoops
(c) ball
(d) motorbike
ladder platform pail (e)
(f) howling A-o-o-o-o

4 Read this magazine article and find the information to complete the poster advertising the Macaroni show.

COME AND SEE THE SHOW!
· ·

The _____ of Michael Macaroni!

A great _____ out!

Don't _____ it!

Macaroni can get out of a straight jacket _____!

See him _____ from a locked chest under water!

No _____ and chain can stop him!

At the _____ Theater for _____ weeks

The Magic of Michael Macaroni

Michael Macaroni is in town with his new show "The Magic of Michael Macaroni." It's the only show in town where you can be sure of having a  great night out. Nobody can escape like Macaroni can. He can get out of a straight jacket in under 20 seconds. No padlock and chain can stop him for more than a minute! He can hold his breath under water for three and a half minutes while escaping from a locked chest in a glass tank of water.

That's the success of Michael Macaroni in his professional life. But he is not so successful in his private life. He can't keep a wife for more than a few months. The present Mrs. Macaroni is asking her husband for a divorce. She is his seventh wife.

"I can't worry about that!" says Macaroni. "I have a job to do and it's a dangerous job."

"The Magic of Michael Macaroni" is showing at the Odeon Theater for two weeks. Don't miss it! It's a great show . . . if you enjoy danger!

5 A Think of a movie you saw recently. Fill in the information in part A of the form. Find a partner and ask him or her questions and fill in the information about your partner's movie in part B of the form.

PART A

Your film:

Actors:

Director:

The story (briefly):

Where the movie is showing:

What is good about the movie:

What is not so good about the movie:

■ ■

PART B

Your partner's film:

Actors:

Director:

The story (briefly):

Where the movie is showing:

What is good about the movie:

What is not so good about the movie:

B Write a short paragraph about either the film you chose or the film your partner chose.

_____

_____

_____

_____

_____

_____

_____

6 B is at a job interview. Complete the conversation.

A: And your _____ name, Mr. Rivas?

B: John.

A: I guess you _____ speak Spanish.

B: Yes.

A: What other languages _____?

B: German—and English, of course.

A: _____ type?

B: Yes, I _____.

A: _____ drive?

B: No, I _____.

A: What _____ in your spare time?

B: I read—mostly novels.

A: _____ is your favorite author?

B: _____.

7 Choose a sports person you admire and write down what he or she can do that you find admirable.

_____

_____

_____

_____

_____

_____

I Have to Pack

1 Solve the clues to complete the vacation crossword.

DOWN

1. Did you take the six-day _____ to Thailand or a four-day one to Korea?

2. What time does our _____ to Hong Kong leave?

3. Our winter vacation starts _____ 16.

4. To be sure of a place on the plane, it is important to _____ your flight.

5. Take your _____ to the check-in.

6. Do you want to stay here in your country for your vacation or do you want to go _____?

ACROSS

1. Let's buy some perfume in the _____-free shop. It's much cheaper.

2. We lost our suitcases, so it's lucky we took out travel _____.

3. Don't carry a lot of cash. It's safer to have traveler's _____.

4. You need a passport and a _____ for Thailand.

5. I'm looking at this vacation _____ so I can decide where to go in the summer.

6. You don't _____ to pick up the tickets. The agency is sending them to the house.

7. You have to have a _____ to travel to another country.

❷ Write the words from the box under the correct headings. Use your dictionary.

TRAIN TRAVEL   PLANE TRAVEL   OCEAN TRAVEL   CAR TRAVEL

_____   _____   _____   _____

_____   _____   _____   _____

_____   _____   _____   _____

track	spare tire	dining car	porthole	harbor	cockpit
deck	windshield	trunk	flight attendant	runway	platform

❸ Listen to the conversation and fill in the notes on the notepad.

Caller:
Business:
Trip:
When:
Flight from:
Flight to:
Have to see:
Have to attend: _____ on _____.
Return flight:
Meeting with Mrs. Henderson about:
Time of meeting:

❹ A Read Margaret's letter to Jill.

Dear Jill,

How are you? How's the family? We're all fine.

I'm writing to find out if you want to come with us on a three-day trip to the log cabin up in Rockville. We're going there on Friday the 10th and driving back on the night of Sunday the 12th. The mountains are really beautiful at this time of year, and the kids would love to have your children come along.

What do you need for a weekend at the cabin? Well, my kids love swimming and there's a lake, so bring bathing suits. I don't have towels at the cabin, so bring some along. It's cold at night, but there are lots of blankets there, so don't worry about those. There are plenty of clean sheets there as well. We like making a fire by the lake and cooking hot dogs and hamburgers, but I think I'll take my small microwave too! It rained last time we went. I hope it doesn't rain this time! Anyway, don't worry about food. We'll take care of that. As a matter of fact, don't bring anything but casual clothes, walking shoes, sweaters for the evening, and good appetites!

We sure hope you can all come along with us. We should have a great weekend. Talk it over with Jack and the kids and call me or write me in the next few days.

Margaret

B Complete Jill's conversation with her husband, Jack.

Jill: I got a letter from Margaret today.
Jack: Yes?

Jill: Yes, she invited us to their _____ in the mountains near Rockville.
Jack: Great! When?

Jill: They're leaving on _____ and driving _____ on _____.

Jack: And what do we have to take?

Jill: Bathing suits because all the kids like _____. Oh, and _____.

Jack: How about food?

Jill: Margaret said not to _____. She's going to take everything.
Jack: What about the weather at this time of year?

Jill: Well, it _____ last time Margaret went, but hopefully it'll be nice this time. We _____ take sweaters, but we _____ take blankets because she keeps a lot of them in the cabin.
Jack: It sounds wonderful.

Jill: Yes, doesn't it? I'll _____ her and tell her we can go!

C Jill likes taking photographs. Here are four photographs of the weekend she spent in Rockville with her husband, Jack, their kids, and her friend, Margaret, and Margaret's family. Jill has stuck the photographs in her album and written something by each one so she doesn't forget the vacation. Complete the sentences.

Here are Jack and the kids going

_____. Rockville

_____ mountains. I'm not _____

picture! I'm _____ photograph!

Mike and Jennifer _____

_____

_____

_____

Here's Jack and Harry. _____

_____

_____

_____

_____

It's raining outside. Margaret and I_____

_____

_____

_____

_____

5 Unscramble the words in column A to make questions. Match the questions to the answers in column.

Column A

1. cold when weather begin does the?

   _____

2. do homework when you do your usually?

   _____

3. your friend when does get up usually best?

   _____

4. cruise when ship does leave the?

   _____

Column B

_____ a. Early, at about 7:00.

_____ b. On Tuesday, August 15th.

_____ c. In October, usually.

_____ d. In the afternoon before I watch TV.

6 Complete these sentences with a phrase from the box.

have to	don't have to	can't

TRAVEL INFORMATION

1. You _____ be at the airport two hours before an international flight during the holiday period, if you want to be sure of your seat.

2. You _____ change planes. You can take a direct flight.

3. Call the consulate and ask if you _____ have a visa for Brazil.

4. When the "No smoking" sign is on, you _____ smoke.

5. You _____ take out travel insurance for the trip, but it's a good idea to do it.

7 A John Teddington is interviewing people to find out about their vacation preferences for the travel agency he works for. At the moment, he's interviewing a woman.

A: Hi, could you answer a few questions for me, please?
B: Sure. It'd be a pleasure.
A: When do you usually take your main vacation?
B: In August.
A: Do you usually travel alone?
B: Oh no! I always go with my husband and our children.
A: What sort of vacation do you like?
B: We like going to the beach.
A: What types of things do you like doing on vacation?
B: Well, I like just relaxing on the beach. The kids love swimming and my husband likes wind-surfing.
A: Okay! That's all. Thank you very much.

B Now question five people in your class. Write a short report: _____

usually takes his vacation in _____, _____

_____

_____

_____

8 Choose one of the following countries: Australia, China, Germany, Kenya, Mexico. Find out what you can about the country (location, weather, language, main products etc.). Prepare a short talk to give to the class. Don't forget pictures!

1 Read the story and number the pictures in the correct order.

Daniela and Joe live in an apartment building downtown. They got married two years ago. They don't have any children yet. Daniela is a fashion designer and Joe is an economist. A month ago, Daniela decided she wanted the apartment completely repainted. They were sitting together on the sofa listening to music after supper when Daniela told Joe of her plans.

"But Daniela!" said Joe. "When they redecorate an apartment it's terrible! There are painters all over! You can't cook because there are people in the kitchen. You can't eat because everything smells like paint. You can't read the newspaper in comfort because there are sheets all over the furniture. You can't even talk because of the workers with cans of paint and ladders listening to your conversation!"

"I'm sure you're exaggerating. But don't worry, honey. We can go away on vacation when they're decorating. That way we don't have to cook! You can read the newspaper in comfort AND we'll have time to talk!"

"Well, O.K.," said Joe, "but how will the decorators get in?"

"We can leave the key with a neighbor," said Daniela.

The next morning at breakfast, Daniela spoke to Joe again about the decorating. "You have to call the decorator today, Joe. I don't have time," said Daniela.

"Right!" said Joe, who was reading the newspaper, drinking coffee, and eating waffles all at the same time. "What do I have to tell him?"

"Well," said Daniela, "I want the living room painted cream with white woodwork. I want light purple walls in the bedroom and dark purple woodwork. Are you listening, Joe? And I'd like the guest room in light yellow."

"O.K.," answered Joe, still reading his newspaper.

"Green woodwork in the guest room, please. Oh, and the kitchen in light blue, with dark blue woodwork."

"Sounds swell," said Joe, finishing his waffles.

"What time is it?" asked Daniela.

"Eight-thirty."

"Oh, I have to go. Don't forget to call the decorator!"

"I won't," promised Joe.

Later that day, Joe called the decorator and arranged everything.

"When do I start?" the decorator asked.

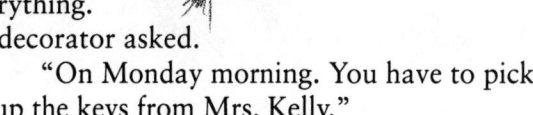

"On Monday morning. You have to pick up the keys from Mrs. Kelly."

"Who is Mrs. Kelly?"

"Our neighbor," explained Joe. On his way home from work in the evening, Joe stopped off at the travel agency to book the vacation.

"How many days do you want at the beach?" asked the travel agent.

"Six days, please," said Joe.

The vacation was a great success: plenty of sun, lots of fun, and a lot of good food. "Now to see our lovely redecorated apartment!" said Daniela as they got home from the beach. Joe opened the door and turned on the light.

What a surprise! "But the living room is painted purple!" said Daniela.

"Isn't that right?" asked Joe nervously.

"No, it is not!" said Daniela. "I told you cream! Let's take a look at the bedroom. Oh no! I wanted light purple with dark purple woodwork! This is blue with yellow woodwork!"

"Let's look at the guest room," suggested Joe.

"Oh, no! It's blue and purple! I told you pale yellow!" Daniela sat down in the kitchen. (It was green and purple.) She felt a little bit sick. "How much did we pay for this?" she asked.

"Don't worry, honey," said Joe cheerfully. "We'll get used to it!"

"Oh, no, Joe. We have to have another six-day vacation."

"Another?"

"Yes. You're going to redecorate the apartment—and I'll just have to read the newspaper to you and talk to you while you work. And if you don't like the smell of paint, you can go on a diet!"

❷ Match the questions in column A with the answers in column B.

Column A

1. Where should we go for our vacation?
2. When does the flight leave?
3. Can she play the piano?
4. Who can play golf?
5. Who is Mr. James?
6. Do you like jazz?
7. What time is it?
8. Who is playing tennis?
9. How many are there?
10. What do you have for breakfast?
11. How much ham would you like?

Column B

A. Yes, I do.
B. It's four-fifteen.
C. Jaime can.
D. At 3:00 in the morning.
E. Coffee and toast.
F. Let's go to the beach.
G. Yes, she can.
H. There are six.
I. Three slices, please.
J. Sylvia and Hans are.
K. He's my father's accountant.

❸ Complete this conversation between two friends talking about a camping trip.

A: We're going camping ___ Saturday. Would you like to come?

B: Yes, but _____ I bring Briana?

A: _____ Briana?
B: She's my cousin.

A: Well, I suppose you can. _____ _____ like camping?

B: Yes, she _____.

A: _____ _____ swim?

B: Yes, she can. _____ _____ people are going?
A: Ten, with Briana. We are going by train to the camp site and staying for three days.

B: _____ does the train leave?

A: _____ 9:30 a.m.
B: O.K. I'll take my guitar.

A: But you _____ play it!
B: That's true, I can't.

A: _____ can play it?

B: Briana. Do we have _____ sleeping bags?

A: No, there are only nine. You _____ take an extra one for Briana.

B: O.K. And do we _____ bring food and drinks?

A: You have to bring food, but you _____ bring drinks. I'm bringing those.

A: _____ food do you want me to bring?
B: Enough for you and Briana for three days.

A: _____ do we come back?

B: _____ Monday afternoon.
A: Great. See you Saturday.

4 Choose a word or phrase from the box to complete these sentences.

much	many	enough	do	does	after
is	are	who	on	at	in
have to	don't have to	mustn't			

1. How many olives _____ there?

2. It's five _____ twelve.

3. Do you have _____ salami for the pizza?

4. _____ Mary like peanuts?

5. How _____ milk do you want?

6. You aren't leaving the country. You _____ take a passport.

7. A: _____ can speak Russian? B: Boris can.

8. You _____ speak in the library. Silence, please!

9. The tour leaves _____ Tuesday.

10. The movie starts _____ 8:00.

11. There _____ a lot of coffee in the kitchen.

12. Don't take cash, take traveler's checks. You _____ be careful.

13. How _____ calories are there in an orange?

14. When _____ you usually leave home?

15. I always take my vacation _____ July.

5 Write true answers to these questions.

1. What time do you get up in the morning? _____

2. What do you have for breakfast? _____

3. Do you like carrots? _____

4. Can you dance? _____

5. Who is your English teacher? _____

6. What do you have to do this week? _____

6 Which word does not belong?

1. October   July   May   Thursday

2. bananas   apples   tomatoes   oranges

3. painting   hockey   soccer   baseball

4. jazz   cello   classical   rock

5. when   where   wheat   who

11 Where's the Health Club?

1 Look at these definitions. What word do they define? All are words from Unit 11 of the student's book.

Example: Food made from flour paste, in various different shapes, and often covered with sauce: ___*Pasta*___ .

1. A room that is heated to high temperatures, especially by steam from burning wood. _____

2. A type of food from India and other parts of south Asia, made of meat and vegetables covered in a thick, often hot-tasting liquid and usually eaten with rice or special bread. _____

3. A wide hall that goes from the entrance to other parts of a hotel. _____

4. An indoor area with wall bars, ropes, and other equipment for exercise. _____

5. A stall on the street or in a station where you can buy newspapers and sometimes magazines and books. _____

6. Sweet food served after the main part of a meal. _____

7. A quite thick, usually cooked, liquid put on or eaten with food. _____

8. A person who is staying in a hotel. _____

9. A piece of equipment needed to send printed material in electronic form along a telephone line. _____

10. Fish and fishlike animals from the sea, especially shellfish, which can be eaten. _____

2 Using your dictionary, match these sets of adjectives with a noun they often describe.

Example: Coffee: strong/weak

I like strong coffee.

I don't like weak coffee.

Column A	Column B
bread	hot/mild
curry	ripe/unripe
steak	stale/fresh
banana	sweet/sour
orange	tough/tender

Say what you do like and what you don't like.

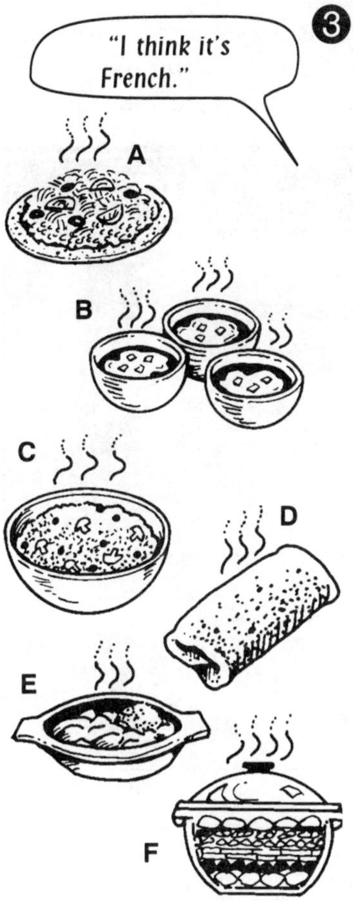

"I think it's French."

A

B

C

D

E

F

❸ Read the descriptions of the following dishes and match them with the drawings. Which countries do you think these dishes are from? Answers on page 45.

_____ 1. This dish, named Lancashire Hot Pot, combines lamb and oysters! You also need onions and potatoes and lambs' kidneys. Alternate layers of potatoes, lamb, onion, kidneys, and oysters are put into a dish and cooked in an oven. The top layer is potatoes. The result is surprisingly good!

_____ 2. This is an excellent dish to eat with chicken or veal. The main ingredients are rice and peas, but you can add other vegetables, such as green beans, chopped carrots, or small mushrooms. You mix in plenty of Parmesan cheese. Delicious!

_____ 3. For this dish, you need fried, crisp corn tortillas. The tortillas are topped with some refried beans and lots of shredded lettuce, tomato, onion, and cheese. They are served with a hot chili sauce. Eat them with your fingers.

_____ 4. This dish is made with pieces of chicken. They are in a curry sauce, which you can have mild or hot. You eat it with chapattis or rice.

_____ 5. The secret of making good onion soup is to fry the onions very slowly until they are golden brown. The soup is served in individual bowls with a lot of Gruyere cheese and squares of dry toast.

_____ 6. This dish is made from shrimp, pork, mushrooms, green onion, red pepper, cabbage, and soy sauce, among other ingredients. Everything is mixed together and then put in an egg roll wrapper. The wrappers are carefully rolled around the filling and the corners are folded in. The rolls are then fried for a short time.

❹ A 🎧 Listen to the description of some new passengers on the Blue Horizons Cruise ship. Look at the list of facilities on the ship. Each of the passengers is particularly interested in one facility. What question does each ask when he or she first boards the ship?

???

Example: *Wanda Menke: Where's the restaurant?*

Sami Obbo _____

Trond Hansen _____

Anita Pratap _____

Jacques Poirier _____

Helen Chang _____

fax	pools	ship's doctor	beauty salon
gym	cinema	disco	duty-free
	stores	restaurants	

B Choose one of the characters from exercise 3. This person is not satisfied with the services and facilities on the ship. Complete this letter of complaint to the ship's captain. Look at the ideas box before you start.

Ideas	Ideas	Ideas	Ideas

Two things you are not satisfied with:

What you can't do because of this:

How you feel about it:

What you think the captain has to do:

The Captain
The Blue Horizon

Dear Captain,

I am writing to _____

_____

_____

_____

_____

_____

Yours sincerely,

5 Complete the dialogue. Jan and James are at a restaurant.

Jan: I can't read the menu. _____ _____ my glasses?
James: They're probably in your bag.
Jan: Oh yes, here they are!

Waiter: Are you ready to _____?
Jan: Yes, we are.

Waiter: _____ would you like to start?

Jan: I'll have _____ chicken noodle soup.
James: Me too.
Waiter: And to follow?

James: Do you have _____ fish?
Waiter: Yes, barbecued or with cheese sauce?
James: Barbecued, please.

Jan: I'll have the chili crab with stir-fry _____.

Waiter: I'm afraid we don't have _____ left.

Jan: Oh, dear. Then I'll have _____ beef curry.

Two hours later. . . .

James: Here's the check. Let me see . . . $25. _____ _____ my wallet?
Jan: At home, probably!

6 A Work with a partner. You want to go on a Caribbean cruise. Person A
looks at the box below; person B looks at the box on page 65. Ask your
partner questions to complete the information about the tour.

How many days is the tour?

*Where does the ship visit? How
do you spell that? Where is that?*

Box A

> Departure date: May 25
> Number of days: 6
> Cost: $2,000 per person
>
> Towns visited: _____ in _____
>
> _____ in _____
>
> _____ in _____
>
> _____ in _____
>
> _____ in _____
>
> _____
>
> _____

B With the information you have, write a short description of the tour.
The tour leaves _____

_____

_____

_____

_____

_____

_____

7 Write a short description of a dish (as in exercise 3) from a particular
country. Read it to the class. Can they guess what country the dish is
from?

1 = Britain, 2 = Italy, 3=Mexico, 4=India, 5=France, 6=China

12 How Was Your Week?

1 A 🎧 Listen to the conversations and write in the missing words below.

Do you have a_____, Janet?
Yes, I do.

Where did you go on your _____?

Oh, we went to a _____.

Did you _____?

Yes, it was _____. That was _____ ago!

Do you have a _____?

No, I don't. I have a _____!
Oh. Where did you meet her?

At _____.

Where did you go on _____?

B Interview three or four people in the class in the same way. Find out if they enjoyed their first date. Why or why not?

2 Unscramble the words in Column A to make verbs. Write the past tense forms of the verbs in Column B. Write a sentence using each verb in the past tense in Column C.

A	B	C
ysat	_stay_	_stayed_	_We stayed for 3 days._
erha	_____	_____	_____
tduys	_____	_____	_____
acll	_____	_____	_____
og	_____	_____	_____
aylp	_____	_____	_____
adre	_____	_____	_____
tivsi	_____	_____	_____
hwtac	_____	_____	_____
sue	_____	_____	_____

3 A Match each verb in Column A with its opposite in Column B. Use a dictionary if necessary.

Example: open/close

Column A	Column B
buy	pass
work	save
leave	sell
send	give
laugh	receive
spend	play
take	cry
fail	arrive

B Complete these sentences with a verb from Column A. You can find the past tenses on page 136 of the student book.

1. They _____ much too much money last weekend.

2. I _____ a new dress yesterday.

3. He was unhappy because he _____ the exam.

4. We paid for the coffee and _____ the restaurant.

5. They _____ a letter to the lawyer last week.

4 A Read this extract from a book that is being made into a movie.

The day after the police officer's visit, Dan moved out of his apartment and he found a room on the fourth floor of an apartment building on the corner of 59th Street and 4th Avenue. He didn't go to work. He didn't call his wife or children, but he missed them. Nobody visited him. Every day he lay in bed until eleven or twelve. Then he got up and went to the diner on the next block and drank a cup of strong black coffee. Sometimes he ate a burger and french fries, but not often. He usually just drank coffee. He never spoke to anybody. Most afternoons he went to the park and sat on a bench. He usually sat near the paddling pool where the children came to sail their model boats. He didn't notice the children. He didn't talk to them. He sat and watched the street and the jewelry store. He just sat there and watched. Sometimes, he wrote something in his notebook. Usually in the evening he went to the movie theater on 4th, only a couple of blocks from the apartment where he lived. He went alone. By ten o'clock he was always back in his room.

Then one day, the janitor at the apartment building saw a photograph of Dan in the newspaper. "Wanted for robbery" said the words under the photograph. The janitor immediately called the police, and some police officers came to the building, but Dan was not there, and he didn't return to his room again. The officers came back to ask questions.

B Here is part of the screenplay of the movie. The police officers are asking questions. Write the missing part of the script.

C Three weeks later, Dan was seen in another town by the manager of a hotel. Write the scene from the film where the officer is questioning the manager about Dan. Use the notes in the officer's notebook for ideas. Work with a partner and then act out the scene for the rest of the class.

- alone
- large suitcase
- dinner in restaurant
- lobster and champagne
- later a woman and three
  children arrived
- stayed two days
- all left together August 18,
  morning
- large car

5 Give advice to these people:

1. I love pastries, but I'm getting fat.

   _____

2. I have a toothache.

   _____

3. I feel so tired!

   _____

4. I have a math test tomorrow and I got a really low grade last month.

   _____

5. I like jogging, but I have a heart condition.

   _____

6. I love pop music and I always have my CD player on really loud, but my neighbors don't like it.

   _____

7. Diana doesn't have a partner for the dance and I'm going alone.

   _____

8. There's a party tonight, but I have an important meeting at 8:30 tomorrow.

   _____

6 Keep a personal diary for one week. Every night write a brief account of what you did during that day. Read your list to a partner. Did you do similar things?

Reading the Future

1 Dianarella is a princess. She wants to know what will happen to her in the future, so she goes to visit a fortune teller.

A 🎧 What does the fortune teller tell Dianarella about her future? Listen and fill in the blanks.

Dianarella _____ a rich prince. One day soon she _____ a frog and she _____ it. The frog _____ into a handsome prince.

B The princess doesn't want to listen to the fortune teller. Dianarella says two things. What are they?

1. I am not _____ the fortune teller.

2. _____ palace.

C What is the problem Dianarella faces?

She _____
_____
_____
_____
_____
_____
_____

2 Dianarella was very upset after her visit to the fortune teller, so she went back to the palace and wrote a letter to her grandmother to tell her about the visit. Complete her letter.

Dear Grandmother,
This morning I went to visit a _____. I asked her about my
_____. She says I _____ looked
a prince. I wanted to know what the _____! My future
like. Guess what she said! A _____ a
is that some day soon _____ a prince! Imagine kissing a
frog and it _____! Of course, I ran out of the room. And
then something awful happened. In the garden I saw a
_____, so I kissed _____. But it didn't turn into a
_____ and the fortune teller said, "You're
_____ frogs before you
meet the right one!" Oh Grandmother, I am so unhappy
here at the palace. Can I come and stay with you at your
castle for a few days?
Love,
Dianarella

Write Grandmother's answer to Dianarella.

_____

_____

_____

_____

_____

_____

_____

❸ A Read the passage and put the pictures in the correct order.

When you find frogspawn in a river or pond, it's hard to believe that one
day it will turn into frogs. Frogspawn looks like gelatin with little black
spots in it. If you find frogspawn, keep it in water in an aquarium. In
several days the black spots in the frogspawn will develop into tadpoles.
At first tadpoles are very small. They look like little black fish and they
can swim very fast. You must get some of the green water plants from the
pond or river. That's what tadpoles eat. In about a week the tadpoles will
be quite big, with long tails. In about five weeks, they'll start to grow
back legs, but they'll still have their tails. By about seven weeks, the back
legs will be long, and short front legs will start to grow. By nine weeks
the tadpoles' tails will disappear and the tadpoles will be frogs. They
won't swim all the time anymore. They'll sit on rocks most of the day
and they'll breathe oxygen like other land animals.

    If you ever have the chance, take some frogspawn home. You'll have
fun watching the frogs develop. There's only one problem: What are you
going to do with the full-grown frogs?

B Using the pictures, write a short account of what will happen to frogspawn.

Keep frogspawn in water in an aquarium. After a few days, black spots will

_____

_____

_____

_____

④ Ask five people in your class what they are going to do after class. Write down their answers.

	Name	Activity
1.		
2.		
3.		
4.		
5.		

⑤ What do you think the world will be like in a hundred years? Discuss in groups.

⑥ A Complete this conversation:

Joyce: What are you _____ do tonight?

Bob: I _____ do my French homework. And then I

_____ watch a movie.

Joyce: Oh, in that case I _____ stay at home too.

B Choose an ending from Column B to complete the suggestions in Column A.

Column A	*Column B*
1. Let's play	a. to the movies.
2. Let's go	b. at home this evening.
3. Let's watch	c. Ben to the party.
4. Let's eat	d. the ball game on TV.
5. Let's invite	e. tennis on Sunday.

7 A Find the verbs in the puzzle and circle them. There are 10.

```
I  N  V  I  T  E  X  S
D  D  I  B  H  A  V  E
F  P  S  V  V  T  M  E
Y  L  I  S  T  E  N  B
F  A  T  G  M  B  U  Y
R  Y  Z  G  O  M  Z  Y
W  P  W  A  T  C  H  B
```

B Now write six suggestions, using six of the verbs in the puzzle.

1. Let's _____

2. _____

3. _____

4. _____

5. _____

6. _____

8 Find out about an important international meeting, convention, or other event (Olympics, ecology summit, a big concert, etc.) that is going to happen in the near future. Which countries are going to send representatives? What will the representatives discuss, do, and so on? Write a report to post on the class bulletin board.

Because I Was Busy

1 Answer the clues to solve the crossword.

ACROSS

1. _____ call an ambulance.

2. _____ you make me a cup of tea?

3. _____ for me here. I'll be back in five minutes.

4. In unit 14 you learned how to make _____.

5. I'm _____, I can't help you.

6. _____ _____! I want to tell you something.

7. Please _____ a fax to Miss Henderson.

8. Could you make some phone calls and _____ these documents?

DOWN

1. Please _____ _____ the car at 6:00. It's at Mom's house.

2. Silvia isn't in class today _____ she is sick.

3. A: _____ were you late last night? B: I got lost.

4. _____ the letter to Mr. French and then give it to me, please.

5. Good afternoon. _____ _____ and sit down.

6. Could you _____ the letters on the way home?

❷ Use your dictionary to place the phrases in the box under the correct heading.

office	hairdresser	restaurant	doctor's office
_____	_____	_____	_____
_____	_____	_____	_____
_____	_____	_____	_____

> It's fractured. ■ Do you have a reservation? ■ Could you pass the stapler, please? ■ Is there any Italian dressing? ■ The stamps and envelopes are in the drawer. ■ Where's the comb? ■ Is there any spray? ■ Where's the pain? ■ Are there any paper clips? ■ Trim the bangs, please. ■ You'll need a prescription. ■ The check, please.

❸ A Complete this conversation with an appropriate word or phrase from the box. Some words must be used more than once. It's Sunday morning and James is talking to his nine-year-old son, Pete.

why	because	put away	could
buy	go	turn off	wear	take

James: _____ the TV and _____ those video games in the closet, Pete.

Pete: _____?

James: _____ Aunty Florence and Uncle Brian are coming over. And _____ you get dressed, please. It's 11:30! Could you _____ your nice brown sweater?

Pete: _____?

James: _____ it was a present from Aunty Flo on your last birthday. And then _____ down to the store and _____ some cookies, and please _____ you take the dog with you.

Pete: _____?

James: _____ he needs the exercise.

B Work with a partner. It is Sunday morning. Some friends are coming over for lunch. The house is a mess. There is no food in the house. Write a short dialogue similar to the one in 3 (A). A makes some requests. B keeps asking "Why?" Act out your conversation to the rest of the class.

4 🎧 Listen to the interviews. Four people are giving reasons for doing what they are doing. Write down their reasons in the places provided below. Compare your answers with those of a classmate.

Daisy and Ben Scarf
Why do they come here on Friday nights?

1. _____
_____
2. _____
_____
3. _____
_____

Alex Kensworth
Why does she do this dangerous job?

1. _____
_____
2. _____
_____

Benny Potts
Why is he helping to save the birds?

1. _____
2. _____

5 **A** Read this article, which tells you how to help kids with homework. What do you think of the advice in this article? Which do you think are the two best tips, and which are the two worst tips? Do you have any trouble completing your homework? Do you have any tips to add?

Good tips: _____
_____

Useless tips: _____
_____

My tips (if you have any to add)_____

It's Wednesday afternoon at the Goodwins' house. Everyone is settling down to do his or her homework.

Having a study schedule for homework is very important, but many families don't know the importance of good study skills, according to Jerome Plant, a former teacher who has written three books on learning. Plant offers these tips on how be a happy and successful student and homework doer:

- Plan your study time. When you get home, decide when you will do your homework. Calculate how long it will take you.
- Do your homework in a comfortable place with enough light. Use a desk, and sit in a comfortable chair.
- Never do your homework in front of the TV or when listening to music.
- Do you want to improve your memory? Stop eating sugar and don't drink coffee. They are the enemies of memory. Take vitamin B—it's a friend of memory.
- Use note cards when you study. Write down the important things you have to remember on the cards. It helps you to remember.
- Never do your homework on the bus on the way to school, or two minutes before the class starts.

B Choose one of these sentences and finish it:

Homework is a waste of time because _____

_____

Homework is useful because _____

6   Keep a record of all the homework you do for the next seven days.

Day _____   **Time started** _____   **Time finished** _____

Type of homework _____   **Place** _____

Comments _____

_____

Day _____   **Time started** _____   **Time finished** _____

Type of homework _____   **Place** _____

Comments _____

_____

Day _____   **Time started** _____   **Time finished** _____

Type of homework _____   **Place** _____

Comments _____

_____

Day _____   **Time started** _____   **Time finished** _____

Type of homework _____   **Place** _____

Comments _____

_____

Day _____   **Time started** _____   **Time finished** _____

Type of homework _____   **Place** _____

Comments _____

_____

Day _____   **Time started** _____   **Time finished** _____

Type of homework _____   **Place** _____

Comments _____

_____

Day _____   **Time started** _____   **Time finished** _____

Type of homework _____   **Place** _____

Comments _____

_____

1 **A** There's a long weekend coming up. Look at these pictures and guess where (a) Ted and his family and (b) Philip are going to go, how they are going to travel, and what they're going to do.

I think Ted and his family _____   I think Philip _____

_____   _____

_____   _____

_____   _____

_____   _____

It was Thursday. Ted and Philip were in the cafeteria of the office where they worked. They were sitting together having lunch. The next day was a Friday, but it wasn't a working day. It was a holiday.

"Well, Ted," said Philip, "where are you going to go for the long weekend?"

"I don't know," said Ted. "Nowhere very special. You can't go far with young kids, and going away with the family gets expensive. I guess we'll go camping in the mountains, if the weather's good."

"That sounds like hard work to me! I'm not married, you know," said Philip. "No kids! No money problems! I'm going to fly to the coast. I'm going to spend three days on the beach. I'm going to swim, lie in the sun, get a tan, play tennis maybe. That's what I call a vacation. It'll be great! Do you want to come?"

"Love to," said Ted, "but . . . it'll be too expensive for the four of us."

Philip laughed. "I'll think of you camping when I'm at my luxury hotel overlooking the ocean," he said.

"Time to get back to work!" said Ted.

The next day came. The weather was lovely. Ted and his wife put the camping things into the car. They packed a good supply of food and drinks. Finally, they strapped the children into their car seats and took the freeway to the mountains.

Philip called a taxi and told the driver to take him to the airport. But when he arrived, there was bad news. There was an airline strike. Philip

went to the other airline counters. He tried to change his ticket for a flight with another airline. But it was a vacation weekend. Everybody was going to the beach! There wasn't a single seat on any flight. There was nothing Philip could do.

The following Monday, Ted and Philip were back at work. They were sitting at the same table having lunch.

"Well, Philip," said Ted, "how was your long weekend at the beach?"

"What long weekend at the beach?" sighed Philip. "There was a strike. The plane didn't take off! I didn't go anywhere! Did you go camping?"

"Yes, we did," said Ted. "It was great! You should come camping with us one day! It's cheap. It's easy. It's fun."

"Yes," said Philip, "and you don't have to take a plane!"

B Write two short paragraphs, one about what happened to Ted and one about what happened to Philip on the weekend.

Ted and his family _____

_____

_____

Philip _____

_____

_____

_____

❷ Answer the clues to solve the puzzle. 1 DOWN is a place where you can buy newspapers.

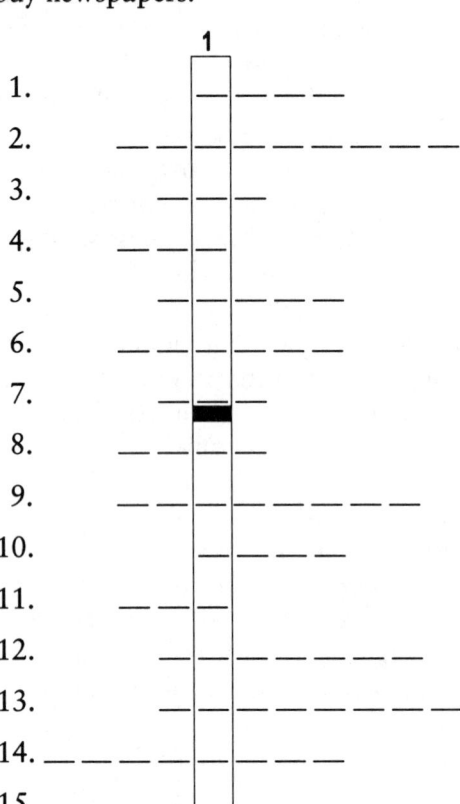

1. I want _____ cheese and brown bread, but I don't want any butter.

2. In the morning I went shopping and in the _____ I stayed home.

3. Yesterday I _____ lunch with my Dad.

4. A: When did you meet John? B: I _____ him in 1992.

5. A: Let's play tennis! B: No, I'm too _____. I want to rest.

6. What a terrible cough! You _____ see a doctor!

7. I'm sorry, but we don't have _____ apple pie.

8. Yesterday we _____ to the movies at 8:30.

9. A: How would you like your eggs? Fried? B: I'd prefer a cheese _____, please.

10. Where _____ you be in 10 years?

11. He _____ in the gym when his wife arrived.

12. What do you _____ do on Saturday nights?

13. There is a tall, dark _____ in your future.

14. You have a _____. You should visit the dentist.

15. On Saturday I walked the dog, I _____ my room, and I washed the dishes.

16. She's a fortune teller. She can _____ the future.

3 Which word doesn't belong? Why?

July, because it's not a day of the week.

Example: Saturday   Thursday   (July)   Sunday

1. gym   waiter   operator   hotel doctor

2. in   go   on   near

3. apple pie   egg salad   fruit salad   nut cake

4. had   worked   went   do

5. great   handsome   fabulous   tired

6. should   Talk!   Stand!   Sit!

4 Complete the sentences with the words in the box.

where	some	because	any	on	will
why	going to	could	shouldn't		

1. _____ you open the window, please?

2. **A:** _____ is the dictionary?

3. **B:** It's _____ the top shelf.

4. Is there _____ water left in the bottle?

5. I _____ eat this cheesecake. I'm overweight.

6. I'm tired. I think I _____ go to bed early tonight.

7. **A:** _____ are you wearing a sweater?

8. **B:** _____ I'm cold.

9. I'd like _____ cheese on my pasta, please.

10. What are you _____ do tomorrow?

❺   Complete these sentences. Look at the example.

Example: I usually go to bed early, but yesterday I went to bed late.

1. I usually study in my bedroom, but yesterday _____.

2. We usually watch TV in the evening, but yesterday _____.

3. They often go to the beach, but last vacation _____.

4. She is usually happy, but yesterday _____.

5. He often has lunch with the family, but yesterday _____.

6. I almost always stay with my uncle when I'm in New York, but on my last trip _____.

❻   Match Column A and Column B.

Column A	Column B
1. Will I ever have a car?	a. I'm sorry, it's too heavy.
2. Why did he leave?	b. Yes, I am, but first I'm going to the bank.
3. Are you going to have lunch with me?	c. It's on the floor.
4. Could you help me move the desk?	d. Maybe next year.
5. Let's go to Paris.	e. He felt ill.
6. Where's the menu?	f. But I hate big cities!

For exercise 4B, page 26.

For exercise 4B, page 26.

INFORMATION BOX B

This is what you have in your kitchen:

    1 package of granola
    5 apples
    1 bag of brown sugar
    1 banana

You want to make cheese and tomato sandwiches for 20 people.
This is what you need. Find out if your partner has the ingredients.

    40 slices of bread
    1 stick of butter
    10 tomatoes
    400 grams of cheese

For exercise 6A, page 45.

Box B

Departure date: _____

Number of days: _____

Cost: _____

Cruise ship visits: Willemstad (Curaçao), Fort de France (Martinique), Saint John's (Antigua), George Town (Cayman Islands), and San Juan (Puerto Rico).

_____

_____